GIRAFFES

Published by Creative Education, Inc., 123 South Broad Street, Mankato, Minnesota 56001

Printed by permission of Wildlife Education, Ltd.

ISBN 0-88682-334-X

GIRAFFES

Created and Written by
John Bonnett Wexo

Zoological Consultant
Charles R. Schroeder, D.V.M.
Director Emeritus
San Diego Zoo &
San Diego Wild Animal Park

Scientific Consultants
Anne Innis Dagg, Ph.D.
Wildlife Biologist, Consultant,
and Freelance Writer

J. Bristol Foster, Ph.D.
Ecological Reserves Unit
Ministry of Lands, Parks
and Housing
Victoria, B.C. Canada

John Harris, Ph.D.
Department of Paleontology
Los Angeles County Museum of
Natural History

Creative Education

Art Credits

Pages Eight and Nine: John Daugherty *(Colorado State University);* **Pages Ten and Eleven:** Walter Stuart; **Page Twleve: Top,** John Francis; **Lower Right,** Pamela Stuart; **Page Thirteen: Upper Right,** Karl Edwards; **Middle Left,** Karl Edwards; **Lower Right,** John Francis; **Page-Sixteen: Lower Left,** John Francis; **Pages Sixteen and Seventeen: Center,** Karl Edwards; **Page Seventeen: Upper Right,** John Francis; **Page Eighteen: Lower Left,** Walter Stuart; **Pages Eighteen and Nineteen:** Mark Hallett; **Page Twenty:** Walter Stuart; **Page twenty-one: Upper Right,** Pamela Stuart; **Lower Left,** Walter Stuart.

Photographic Credits

Cover: Willard Luce *(Animals Animals);* **Pages Six and Seven:** Norman Lightfoot; **Page Twelve: Upper Right,** Peter Davey *(Bruce Coleman, Inc.);* **Lower Left,** Fawcett *(Animals Animals);* **Lower Right,** Mark Newman *(Animals Animals);* **Page Thirteen: Upper Right,** Des Bartlett *(Bruce Coleman, Ltd.);* **Lower Left,** George Holton *(Photo Researchers);* **Pages Fourteen and Fifteen:** Fawcett *(Animals Animals);* **Page Sixteen: Upper Left,** Z Leszczynski *(Animals Animals);* **Upper Right,** Zoological Society of San Diego; **Center,** Fran Allan *(Animals Animals);* **LowerRight,** Reinhard Kunkel *(Peter Arnold, Inc.):* **Page Seventeen: Upper Left,** Joe McDonald *(Bruce Coleman, Ltd.);* **Lower Right,** Carol Hughes *(Bruce Coleman, Ltd.);* **Page Nineteen: Upper Right,** Courtesy of Field Museum of Natural History, Chicago; **Lower Right,** F. Vollmar *(Bruce Coleman, Inc.);* **Page Twenty:** Philadelphia Museum of Art; Given by John T. Dorrance; **Page Twenty-one: Upper Left,** Charles Van Valkenburgh/Wildlife Education, Ltd.; **Lower Right,** Anthony Bannister; **Page Twenty-two and Twenty-three:** Simon Trevor/D.B. *(Bruce Coleman, Inc.).*

Our Thanks To: Mrs. Virginia Erwin; Mrs. Paquita Machris; Valerie Stallings; Dr. David Fagan; Lynnette Wexo.

Creative Education would like to thank Wildlife Education, Ltd., for granting them the rights to print and distribute this hardbound edition.

Contents

Giraffes are the tallest of all land animals. Most of their great height comes from their long necks and long legs. Giraffe necks are so long that the animals can reach high up into trees to feed on leaves. And their legs are so long that they can take huge steps when they walk or run.

Strange as it may seem, the origin of the giraffe's name had nothing to do with the animal's size. It was the giraffe's *speed* that gave it its name. The word "giraffe" comes from the Arab word *xirapha* (ZEE-RAF-AH), which means "the one that walks very fast."

Giraffes live in Africa. But they are only found in certain parts of that continent. You will usually see giraffes on tree-dotted plains, or in open forests, where the trees are not too close together. You will almost never see them in deserts or in dense forests.

Giraffes are plant-eaters, or herbivores (HERB-UH-VORZ). Their favorite foods are the leaves of trees. And for this reason, they like to live where there are plenty of trees. But giraffes also try to stay away from places where they can't see lions coming. And they like to be sure that they can run away when a lion does come. So they stay out of thick forests, where the tangled branches might get in their way.

Sometimes, giraffes wander a great deal in search of food. Often, they spend only a few minutes eating at one tree before going on to an-

other. Moving from tree to tree, a giraffe can walk hundreds of miles in a few months.

Most of the animals that live on the African plains must go to a waterhole or stream every day to drink. But not the giraffes. They get most of the moisture they need from the green leaves that they eat. In a certain way, this makes the life of a giraffe safer, because waterholes are risky places. Lions and other predators often wait there to attack animals as they drink. So the less a giraffe has to go for water, the safer it is.

Groups of giraffes are called herds. But giraffe herds are different from the herds of most other animals. For one thing, members of a giraffe herd don't have to stay with that herd if they don't want to. They are free to wander off at any time and join another herd. For another thing, the structure of a giraffe herd is so loose that it's often hard to tell who the leader is.

Herds are usually small, but herd size may depend on the amount of food that's available. If there's more food in a certain area, you might find more giraffes there. At times, the "herd" may include only two giraffes. At other times, more than 50 of them gather together.

Adult male giraffes are called bulls. Adult females are called cows. And a young giraffe of either sex is called a calf. Giraffes can live a long time. The oldest giraffe on record lived to be almost 28 years old.

Giraffes from different parts of Africa

have different color patterns. Because of this, people used to think that there were many different kinds of giraffes. But today, we know that there is only one kind (or SPECIES) of giraffe. Their skins may look different, but under the skin all giraffes are pretty much the same.

Still, the color patterns are useful if you want to know what part of Africa a giraffe comes from. For example, if you see a giraffe with large dark spots that are very close together, it is a reticulated (REH-TICK-u-lay-tid) giraffe. And reticulated giraffes are only found in East Africa. (See if you can find the reticulated giraffe on the map.)

KORDOFAN GIRAFFE
Giraffa camelopardalis antiquorum

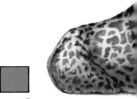

ANGOLAN GIRAFFE
Giraffa camelopardalis angolensis

NIGERIAN GIRAFFE
Giraffa camelopardalis peralta

SOUTHERN GIRAFFE
Giraffa camelopardalis giraffa

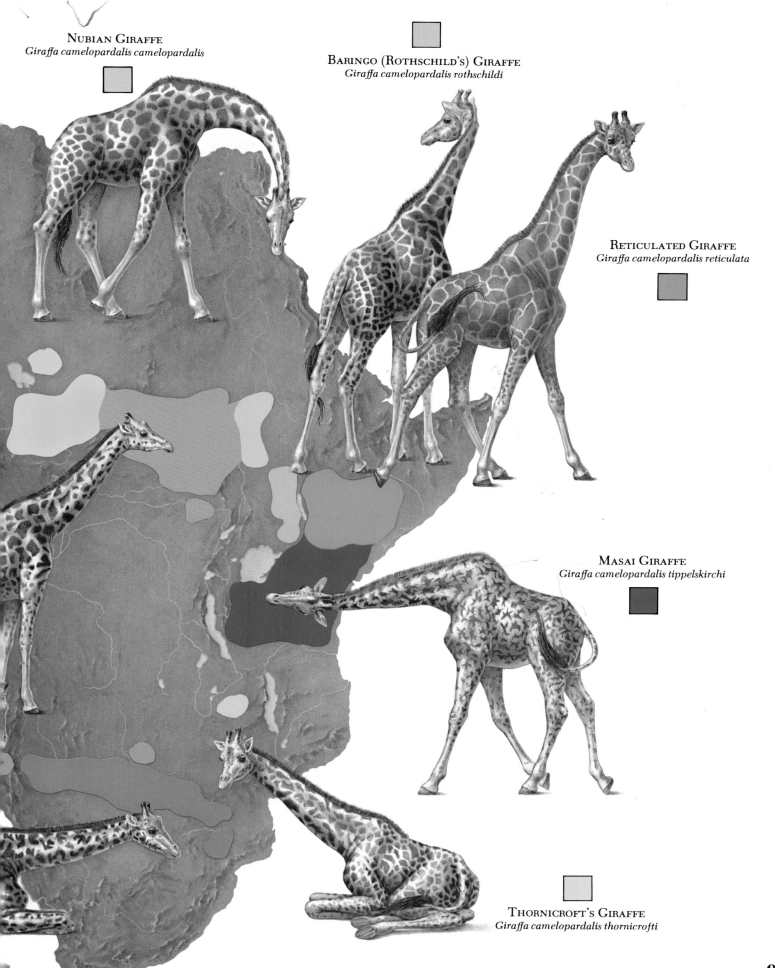

Nubian Giraffe
Giraffa camelopardalis camelopardalis

Baringo (Rothschild's) Giraffe
Giraffa camelopardalis rothschildi

Reticulated Giraffe
Giraffa camelopardalis reticulata

Masai Giraffe
Giraffa camelopardalis tippelskirchi

Thornicroft's Giraffe
Giraffa camelopardalis thornicrofti

The neck of a large giraffe can be 6½ feet long (198 centimeters). And its tail can be even longer—up to 6 feet 8 inches (203 centimeters), when you include the 3-foot tassel of hair on the end.

When most animals run, their rear legs do most of the pushing. But giraffes are different. When they run, the *front* legs do most of the pushing. This is one reason why they have such large muscles in their shoulders.

Everything about a giraffe is BIG.

Adult male giraffes are usually about 17 feet tall (5.2 meters), and they can weigh as much as 3,000 pounds (1,360 kilograms). The largest male on record was over 19 feet tall (5.8 meters).

The heart of an adult giraffe can be over two feet long (61 centimeters). It can pump 20 gallons of blood (76 liters) *every minute*. Giraffes have four stomachs, and a large male probably eats about 75 pounds of food (34 kilograms) a day. When a giraffe drinks, it can take in 10 gallons of water (38 liters) at one time.

Females are smaller than males—but still very large. An average female is over 14 feet tall (4.3 meters). And the largest female on record was almost 17 feet tall (5.2 meters).

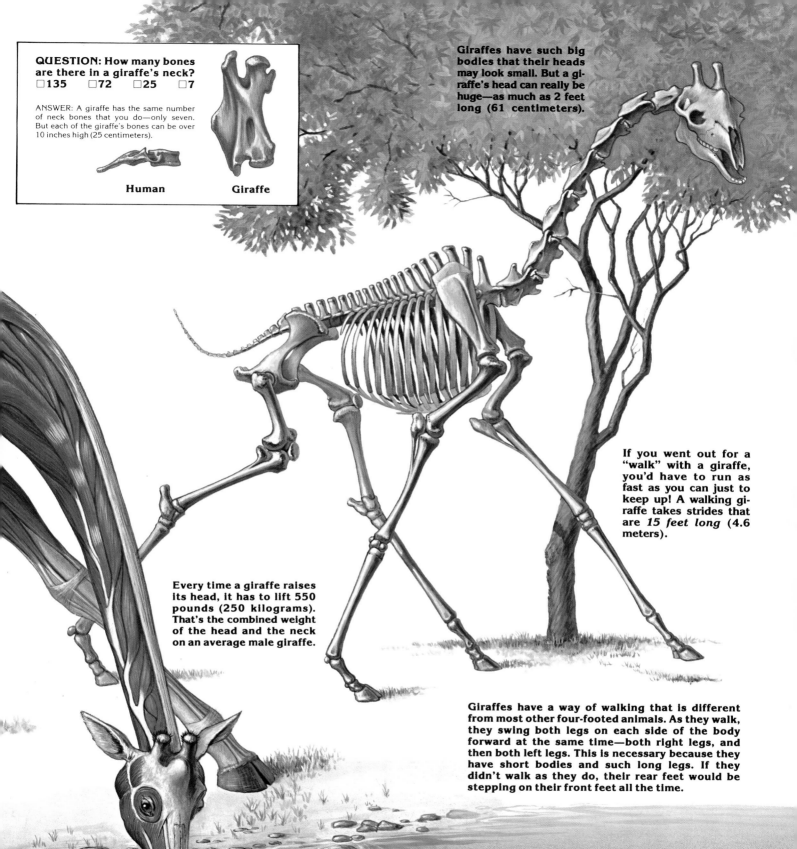

QUESTION: How many bones are there in a giraffe's neck?
☐ 135 ☐ 72 ☐ 25 ☐ 7

ANSWER: A giraffe has the same number of neck bones that you do—only seven. But each of the giraffe's bones can be over 10 inches high (25 centimeters).

Human

Giraffe

Giraffes have such big bodies that their heads may look small. But a giraffe's head can really be huge—as much as 2 feet long (61 centimeters).

If you went out for a "walk" with a giraffe, you'd have to run as fast as you can just to keep up! A walking giraffe takes strides that are *15 feet long* (4.6 meters).

Every time a giraffe raises its head, it has to lift 550 pounds (250 kilograms). That's the combined weight of the head and the neck on an average male giraffe.

Giraffes have a way of walking that is different from most other four-footed animals. As they walk, they swing both legs on each side of the body forward at the same time—both right legs, and then both left legs. This is necessary because they have short bodies and such long legs. If they didn't walk as they do, their rear feet would be stepping on their front feet all the time.

The neck of a giraffe is long enough to reach high into the trees—but it isn't quite long enough to reach down to the ground. When a giraffe wants to drink, it is forced to bend its knees or spread its front legs wide apart (as the giraffe here is doing).

The life of a giraffe is quiet, most of the time. In general, this is because giraffes mind their own business. They don't bother other animals, as a rule. And adult giraffes are so big that other animals don't often dare to bother them.

Lions and a few other predators do attack baby giraffes, and once in a while a group of hunting lions may go after an adult giraffe. At such times, the normally peaceful giraffe can become a fierce fighter, kicking savagely with its huge feet. Mother giraffes defending their babies have been known to kick the heads of lions right off.

Given a choice, however, a giraffe would rather walk (or run) away from trouble. It is remarkable that one of the largest and strongest animals on earth is also one of the most peaceful.

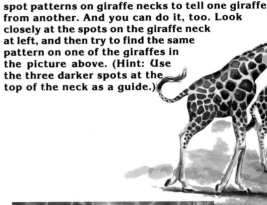

The pattern of spots on every giraffe is unique—different from the patterns on all other giraffes. For this reason, scientists are able to use the spot patterns on giraffe necks to tell one giraffe from another. And you can do it, too. Look closely at the spots on the giraffe neck at left, and then try to find the same pattern on one of the giraffes in the picture above. (Hint: Use the three darker spots at the top of the neck as a guide.)

When a baby giraffe is born, it is already bigger than many fully grown men and women. It may stand over 6 feet tall (1.8 meters), and can weigh 150 pounds (68 kilograms). During the first week of its life, the baby can grow more than *one inch a day* (2.5 centimeters). And by the time it is one year old, it will be almost 10 feet tall (3 meters). Usually, only one giraffe is born at a time. Twins are very rare.

Within an hour after it is born, a baby giraffe is able to stand up and take milk from its mother. For the first year of its life, it may not drink water. Often, it gets all the moisture it needs from milk and the green plants that it eats.

The footprints of giraffes are larger than dinner plates. On an adult male, each foot can be 12 inches long by 9 inches wide (30 centimeters by 23 centimeters).

Cow Foot

Giraffe Foot

Many people think that giraffes don't have voices and can't make sounds like other animals do. But this isn't true. When they are in the mood, giraffes can moo like a cow, bleat like a calf, and bellow like a bull. They can grunt, snort, cough, whistle, and growl. And when they sleep, they sometimes snore. But giraffes are only rarely in the mood to make sounds. They are just quiet by nature.

SNORT!

MOO!

The long legs of giraffes make them good runners—and they make it easy for giraffes to get over walls and fences, too. A large giraffe can easily step over a fence 6 feet high (1.8 meters)...and then run away at a speed of 35 miles per hour (56 kilometers per hour).

In Africa, giraffes are often seen with little birds on their backs. These are called tick birds, because they eat ticks and other insects that may attach themselves to a giraffe's skin. This is good for the birds, because they get fed. And it's good for the giraffes, too, because they are kept cleaner.

Giraffes are like walking lookout towers. Their eyes are so far above the ground that they can usually see what's coming long before any of the other animals see it. In Africa, when a whole group of giraffes turns to stare in one direction, it may be lions they see coming. But in the zoo (as above), it usually means that they see a keeper coming with food.

These mature reticulated giraffes can be found only in East Africa.

Giraffes like to eat. In fact, they spend many hours a day feeding. Usually, they start eating early in the morning. During the hottest part of the day, they rest. And then they may go on eating until late at night.

They don't chew their food much before they swallow it. Instead, they chew it when they are resting in a safe place. At such a time, they bring small amounts of food back up the throat into the mouth, chew it completely, and then swallow it again. This is called "chewing cud," or ruminating (ROO-min-ate-ing).

Giraffes are browsers. This means they eat leaves and buds from trees and bushes, and do not usually eat grass. Their favorite food is acacia leaves (ah-KAY-sha). These plants have big thorns, but the giraffes are able to avoid the thorns as they eat.

In many parts of Africa, the trees have been shaped by giraffes. They eat all the leaves up to a certain height, and this makes the trees look flatter on top.

In nature, animals that live in the same area don't usually eat the same kinds of food. Some animals (like zebras) eat grass that is close to the ground. Others (like gerenuks) eat leaves on low bushes. And giraffes, of course, eat leaves high up in the trees. In this way, the animals don't compete directly for food, and there is usually enough for all.

The "horns" on a giraffe aren't really horns at all. They are bony lumps on the skull, covered with skin and hair. The scientific name for them is ossicones (AH-suh-cones). Giraffes often have more than two ossicones. Some males have as many as five.

A giraffe's tongue can be incredibly long—up to *22 inches long* (56 centimeters)! When feeding, giraffes strip leaves off branches with their tongues. The end of the tongue is dark, and this may be to protect it from the hot sun.

One easy way to tell a male giraffe from a female giraffe is to look at its horns. Males have larger horns than females. And because they use their horns to fight, the hair is usually rubbed off the ends of a male's horns. Females and young males have hair on top of their horns.

Both male and female giraffes have "horns." But only the males seem to have any use for them. Sometimes, two males will have a contest to see which of them is the stronger (or dominant) animal. They stand side by side and hit each other with their horns. They hammer at each other until one of them has had enough and walks (or runs) away. Most of the time nobody gets hurt.

For months after they are born, young giraffes may not go out into open country to feed with the rest of the herd. Their mothers often leave them in a kind of giraffe "kindergarten," where a group of little ones is usually cared for by a single female giraffe.

The only living relative of the giraffe is the okapi (O-KAH-PEE). At first glance, this beautiful animal doesn't look much like a giraffe. It is less than half as tall as a giraffe and has a much shorter neck. But scientists tell us that the okapi looks a lot like ancient relatives of the giraffe that are no longer alive.

In the past, these ancient giraffe relatives lived in many parts of Africa, Europe, and Asia. Some of them were much larger than the okapi, and some were much smaller. At one time or another, many types of giraffe-like animals have lived on earth—but only the giraffe and the okapi are left.

EUROPEAN SIVATHERE
Birgerbohlinia schaubei

EARLIEST KNOWN GIRAFFID
Prolibytherium magnieri

AFRICAN SIVATHERIUM
Sivatherium maurusium

Present Range of the Okapi

"STAG HORN" GIRAFFID
Climacoceras gentryi

The home of the okapi in central Africa was one of the last places to be reached by European explorers. And this is why the okapi was the last big land animal discovered on earth.

For years before it was actually found, native Africans had been telling explorers about a large, striped animal that lived in the dense Congo forest. But no real evidence of the animal's existence was found until 1901. In that year, an English explorer named Sir Harry Johnston saw a native soldier wearing a striped bandoleer (or shoulder strap). Sir Harry bought the bandoleer and started trying to find out where it came from.

Soon, he was able to locate some complete skins and two skulls. And the horns on the skulls made it clear that the mystery animal was a relative of the giraffe. The native name for the animal was "okapi," and this became the scientific name. Several years later, after much searching, a living okapi was finally captured.

Marc Hallett

The okapi and the giraffe, along with all of their ancient relatives, are called giraffids (juh-RAF-idz). The earliest known giraffid lived in North Africa about 15 million years ago. Many of the ancient giraffids had much larger horns than a giraffe or an okapi. The last of the ancient giraffids to die out was probably the Sivatherium (see-va-THEER-ee-um) shown below. Some scientists believe that this animal did not become extinct until 5,000 years ago. A sculpture created at that time in Iraq (shown at right) seems to show a sivatherium.

ASIATIC SIVATHERIUM
Sivatherium giganteum

Although the okapi is related to the giraffe, it is different in many ways. It lives in the forest, for instance, and usually lives alone (except for mothers with babies). Females are larger than males, and only young okapi have manes. Instead of spots, an okapi has a dark coat, with zebra-like stripes on the legs. This color and pattern help to hide the animal in the dark forest.

"HORN-NOSED" SIVATHERE
Giraffokeryx punjabiensis

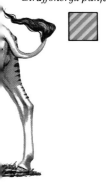

OKAPI
Okapia johnstoni

People have always admired giraffes.

You might say that we humans have always "looked up" to giraffes, because they are so much taller than we are. Like whales and elephants and dinosaurs, their sheer size fills us with wonder and respect. More than that, the odd shape and gentleness of these giants have excited our curiosity.

Long ago, people began trying to explain why giraffes look the way they do. One very old African story said that God made the giraffe after finishing the camel and the leopard. There were some parts left over, so God decided to make an animal that was as big as a camel with spots like a leopard. The ancient Romans believed a similar story and called the giraffe a "camel-leopard." (From this, the giraffe got one of its scientific names: *camelopardalis*.)

Until recently, giraffes were rarely seen outside of Africa. In Europe and Asia, they were so rare and valuable that kings gave them to other kings as gifts. The picture above shows a giraffe that was given to the Emperor of China by the Emperor of India more than 500 years ago.

As long as there have been zoos, giraffes have been popular zoo animals. The first zoo in the world was created 3,500 years ago by Queen Hatshepsut (hat-SHEP-soot) of Egypt. A giraffe was brought 1,500 miles (2,414 kilometers) down the Nile River for the Queen's zoo.

The grace and beauty of giraffes have thrilled people for a very long time. More than 10,000 years ago, an unknown artist painted this scene on the wall of a cave in North Africa.

In some parts of Africa, people believe that giraffe tails are lucky. A bracelet or fly whisk made of the hair from a giraffe's tail is supposed to keep its owner healthy and safe from danger. Luckily for giraffes, this belief is dying out.

Pictures like the one above were probably painted by giraffe hunters, as a kind of magic to bring them good luck in the hunt. Today, bushmen of South Africa still hunt giraffes with bows and arrows, as ancient Africans did.

At times, the human admiration for giraffes may have been carried a little too far. When the first giraffe was brought to Paris in 1827, it nearly caused a riot. People crowded into the streets to see the wonderful animal, and soldiers had to be called out to control them. Before long, "giraffe" fashions began to appear. Women wore their hair in a "giraffe" style. And men's coats had "giraffe" spots on them. For more than a year, Paris was "giraffe crazy."

The future of giraffes may not be quite as dark as the future of many other African animals. For one thing, people really like giraffes and want to help them survive. For another, giraffes really don't give anybody any reasons for hurting them. Unlike some other animals, giraffes do not bother the cattle and other livestock that people raise. And they usually don't eat the crops that people grow. Giraffes stay pretty much out of people's way, and mind their own business.

Unfortunately, it isn't always easy for people to stay out of the way of giraffes. The number of people in Africa is growing so fast that humans and giraffes find themselves in competition for the same living space in many places. More and more people are being born, and they need more land on which to live and raise food. This means that less and less land is available for the trees that giraffes like to eat, and for the giraffes themselves.

The growing number of humans has brought another serious problem with it. There are so many poor and hungry people in Africa that hunting of giraffes is increasing. In most African countries, it is against the law to hunt giraffes. But hungry people kill giraffes anyway, to get the great amount of meat that is on every giraffe. These illegal hunters are called poachers (PO-CHURZ), and it is very hard to stop them.

Inside the great national parks of Africa, there are police that try to protect the giraffes and other animals. But the parks are very big, and the number of police is often very small. Outside the parks, there is usually nobody to protect the giraffes.

Today, there are more than 100,000 giraffes in Africa. Many of these still live outside of the national parks. In the future, however, it seems likely that national parks will be the only places where there will be room for giraffes, and where they will be reasonably safe. Since there is only limited living space within the parks, the number of giraffes in Africa will probably be smaller.

Index

		DATE DUE